How to Write a Business Plan

Business Planning in Plain English

Elliot J. Smith

Copyright 2017 – Elliot J. Smith. All rights reserved.

Printed in the USA

The information in this book represents only the view of the author. As of the date of publication, this book is presented strictly for informational purposes only. Every attempt to verifying the information in this book has been done and the author assumes no responsibility for errors, omissions, or inaccuracies.

Contents

CHAPTER 1 INTRODUCTION TO BUSINESS PLANS 1

CHAPTER 2 WRITING YOUR BUSINESS PLAN 6

CHAPTER 3 BUSINESS PLAN EXAMPLE 39

CHAPTER 4 COMMON MISTAKES TO AVOID 62

CHAPTER 5 CHOOSING A NICHE 78

BUSINESS PLAN TEMPLATE 100

OTHER BOOKS BY ELLIOT J. SMITH 113

Chapter 1

Introduction to Business Plans

So, you have a great idea, and you need a great plan. Either you're developing a brand-new business idea, or you're looking to make major changes within your existing business. Whatever the case may be, you need a plan, and you need a *good* one. Business plans are relevant to virtually every business, regardless of your chosen business model or industry. When you make a business plan, you must ensure that you are creating a plan that you can update as needed, and maintain when markets change, and your company grows.

If you are in the process of getting ready to prepare a business plan, you probably have a few questions. Questioning the process is normal; your time is valuable, and you want to make sure you are investing it in the best way possible. After all, time is money, right? If you have questions regarding what a business plan is and what purpose it serves, you're not alone. Let's take a few minutes to discover exactly what a business plan is and why your business needs one.

What Is a Business Plan?
In short, a business plan is an official business document you will use to convey the action plan for your business. This document has sections to discuss important topics such as business summary, your product or service, what stage of business you're in, information about your target audience, your financial situation, your future projections and more! This important document allows you to summarize your entire business outlook in a single place, making it easy to discover your exact plans and make sure you're staying on track.

Why Do You Need One?
Anytime you want to start a business, you need a plan. If you choose to take your great idea and

convert it into a great business, you need a business plan. This document is important to any business, brand new or existing. If you don't have one, you need one. If you have one, but it is outdated, you must redo it. Having a business plan, especially an up-to-date one, is important for many reasons. The primary reason is that it keeps your business on track. It gives you focus for what you want to achieve and a clear outline of what you must do to succeed. It discusses your strengths and weaknesses, as well as your action plan in important areas such as marketing, employee management, financial management, and more! In addition to being an action plan for you, it is an action plan for your employees. It can help you add employees who will be effective, and ensure that they are clear on what they must accomplish while on the job. Finally, business plans are a must-have if you will be requesting funding of any sort from anyone. A business plan will allow you to convey to creditors that you have thought out your entire business and that you are prepared to repay any loans you receive. When creditors are considering giving you a significant amount of money to start or expand your business, they will want to know that you have a strong action plan and a promising future. A business plan helps you prove that.

How Can I Make Sure It's Great?

A great business plan starts with all the relevant information. In the next chapter, you will discover exactly what information must be included in your business plan. However, to make sure you have a great business plan and not just a completed one, you must take the time to thoughtfully and thoroughly fulfill every category of the plan. Go above and beyond in completing your research and include every relevant piece of information in your business model. In addition to being exhaustive in your research and thorough in your reports, you must ensure that everything is focused and on-topic. All information should be restricted to its relevant category, and if it doesn't directly serve your business plan, it should not be included.

What is a Business Model?

Unlike a business plan, which outlines your action plan for your company, a business model is a model by which you intend to do business. There are many different business models you can use to run your business effectively. Your model will depend partially on your products and services. Once you identify what you are serving to consumers, you can decide which model will help you best reach your market and sell your product or services. Essentially, a model is a design for how you will successfully operate your business. It helps you identify revenue streams, your customer base, what your products must be like, and any relevant details regarding financing needs.

Chapter 2

Writing Your Business Plan

Writing a business plan can seem intimidating. The document can be lengthy, with a lot of information involved, some of which requires you to conduct extensive research and market testing. The best way to create your business plan is to start with the easy parts: the things you already know plenty about. Then you can start conducting research and collecting information for the other areas. Once you fulfill all sections of the business plan, do a thorough proofreading and grammar check, as well as fact check all your information. Review your numbers to ensure they are consistent and that if you are requesting funding with your business plan, you are not requesting more (or less) than you have accounted for.

There are about fourteen areas of your business plan on which you must focus. These areas each require you to take your time and ensure that all the information is accurate and present. You should also stay focused on each section, ensuring it contains no irrelevant information. Rambling on about things that do not concern that specific topic will detract from the professionalism and quality of your business plan. If you have information you feel should be included but that does not directly support the topic about which you are writing, you can include this information in the appendix, which you will learn more about later in this chapter.

Executive Summary

Although this section should be presented first in your business plan, it should be completed last. Completing your executive summary *after* you have completed the rest of your business plan will allow you to ensure that you have clearly summarized everything you have learned. This section is essentially a summary of your entire business plan and business idea. Including this first allows anyone reading your business plan to immediately become aware of what you are doing and what your intentions are. It is a great opportunity to capture people's attention and let them see why you stand apart from the other businesses out there.

Your executive summary should include summarized information for your entire business plan. There are a few things you absolutely must include in this section, such as:

- Mission Statement: Include your company's mission statement. This statement should summarize, in a paragraph or less, the purpose of your business and what you intend to achieve.
- Company Basics: Include basic information about your company, such as when it was founded, who founded it, the founders' roles and involvement in the company, how many employees you have, and your business location.

- Growth Highlights: Brief evidence and information about your company's growth should be included in this section. You should also include financial or market highlights if available. Additionally, you can include charts or graphs to help convey your growth.
- Offers: Your executive summary should have a section in which you highlight what your company offers. This includes any products and services.
- Current Finances: It is important to briefly discuss your current financial situation, especially if you intend to request financial aid. This should include any relevant information regarding your banks and existing investors.
- Outlook: Finally, you must include a brief overview of what your company outlook is and what your intentions are on the future of your company.

By completing this section last, you will have access to the information you collect when researching other sections. Having this information handy will allow you to make this summary specific and informative. The more clear, concise, specific, and informative you are in this section, the more attractive your business plan will be to anyone looking at it.

Products and Services

Many businesses begin because someone had a brilliant idea for a product or service that could fulfill a potentially large need in the market. Since the products and services serve as one of the backbones of the company, it makes sense to have a section dedicated to them in the business plan. In this section, you let your products and services shine. You can share details about what your products are, why they serve your market, how they compare to the competition, and what your intention is with them in the future. If you want to know exactly what information you should include in this section, it is:

- Detailed Description: In this section, you can get specific about your product. Share what makes it shine, why it is so amazing, and what need it fulfills. Write this part from a customer's point of view. Often, businesses think they have landed an incredible product, but fail to see whether it will actually fulfill a true market need. Just because an idea is incredible doesn't mean it will be successful. Make sure you really look at your products and services from a customer's standpoint and express this section from that point of view.
- Lifecycle: Every product has a lifecycle, and you must include this information when talking about your product. Furthermore, you should include what stage of its lifecycle your product is in and what you intend to do when it reaches the end of its lifecycle.
- Intellectual Property: If there is any intellectual property, such as trademarks, copyrights, or patents (even pending) on your product or service, or any other legal agreement

surrounding it, you must discuss that in your business plan.

- Research and Development (R&D): If your company has done any research and development activities (and you should have), include your findings and anything you learned during this process. This will help ensure your product is at the top of its class and that you can prove it. In addition to your own research and development, look at what other companies have discovered in your target industry.

It is important that, even if you are incredibly excited, you keep this section of your business plan focused. While it is OK to let your excitement flow through and use it to express why your product or service is so amazing, you must ensure that you don't ramble on about things that are not relevant to this section. In this section, in particular, this can be easy to do because this is generally the epicenter of the entire business idea and plan. Take your time and make sure everything is clearly stated and that anyone who reads your business plan will understand what it is you are trying to convey.

Current Business Stages

It is important to express what stage your business is in at the time of the writing of your business plan and/or sharing it with others. Whether your business is brand new or rapidly growing and undergoing a major developmental stage, it is important to convey that. You must clearly express what stage you are in, provide a brief history of the business (or of the business idea and how it came to be if you're brand new) and indicate your projection for future development. In this section, you get the opportunity to share a detailed overview of what stage your business is in and where you intend to take it in the next year, and up to the next five years.

Target Market

Next to the product or service, your target market or consumer base is also an important backbone of your company. It is important to get very specific on who your target market is and to express this in your business plan. Having this in your business plan will help you explain to whom you are appealing and why they should be interested in your product. You want to get extremely specific on whom you are looking to target because your unique audience will largely contribute to what your business model looks like. When you are talking about your target market, there are many things you must consider, including:

- Demographics: Who exactly is your target audience? How old are they? Where do they live? What are their interests? What lifestyle do they lead? In the demographics section, you can describe exactly *who* your target audience is. The more focused you get, the easier it will be for you to find your customers!

- Psychographics: What compels your target audience to purchase things? How do they decide whether they need a product? What will attract their interest and what will repel it? The psychographics of your customers helps you understand how they purchase products and what it takes for them to buy something. This important information will help you determine exactly how to market to your audience so that you prompt them to purchase from you.
- Needs: Make sure your product or service is actually going to fulfill a need in the market. To do this, you first need to understand exactly what the audience's needs are. You can do this through basic market research and understanding what types of things they generally buy and how this fulfills a specific need in their lives.
- Niche: When you are figuring out what your target market is, you will have the opportunity to explore your individual niche. Having a niche allows you to promote a specialized

service to a smaller sector of the market – a sector that is most likely to find your product or service appealing. Focusing specifically on this sector will help you greatly when it comes to planning your business model and marketing strategies.

It is important that you get clear on who your target audience is. The more you can understand who they are, what needs they have, and why they will feel that your product or service fulfills their needs, the easier it will be to plan your business model, including marketing strategies. Because your customers are a large part of your business's success, you want to make sure that you invest a great deal of time and effort into understanding exactly who they are and why they should be interested in your product or service.

Target Market Size

In addition to understanding your target market, you must get clear on the size of the market.

Understanding the size provides vital information in many respects: It allows you to gain a realistic idea of how many employees you need, what quantity of products or services you must have available, at which scale your marketing efforts should be made, and how much revenue you can expect to generate as a result of having all these things in place. When you are writing the section of your business plan dedicated to target market size, you must focus on two things: target audience size and expected audience reach.

Target Audience Size

The size of your target audience will be based on what industry you are in and what you are marketing. You can use your target market information to generate a realistic number representing the size of your target audience. Your target audience will include *any* potential client, whether or not they are likely to buy. If they qualify to be a consumer in your industry, they should be considered part of this section.

Expected Audience Reach

Here is where you narrow down and become more realistic. Your company isn't going to appeal to every single consumer in your target audience. While you would like to think it could, the reality is that it won't. So, based on all your research, you must come to a conclusion about how much of your target audience you actually expect to reach. While they might not all turn into loyal customers, these are the people who you think will actually get to see and show some interest in your product. From this section, you will generate consumers – and hopefully loyal ones at that.

Market Plan

After discussing exactly what you are offering and discovering exactly who lies in your target audience, you are ready to create a market plan. Here, you can share your intended strategies when it comes to marketing. You will be discussing information such as method of market entry, intended marketing strategies, and growth sustainability projections. This is where you explain how you are going to promote your product or service to your target audience to gain maximum reach and convert as many leads into consumers as possible. The information you must convey in this section includes:

- Entrance Strategy: How and when you intend to enter the market. If you have already entered the market with a product or service, you must outline how you intend to refresh the market with your new strategies.
- Growth Strategies: What methods you intend to use to promote internal and external business growth. In this section, you want to include how you will use your marketing strategies to increase the number of consumers and continue growing your sales volume. You will also include how you intend to add employees and new locations, as well as other important growth sustainability factors to maintain your growth from the inside.

- Distribution Channels: This includes all the methods through which you intend to distribute your products or services. You can do this through independent sellers, selling wholesale/on consignment, online sales, or other selling methods. You can even combine several methods. However, you choose to distribute your products or services; you must include that information here.
- Communication Strategy: This involves the exact promotional tools you will use to share your products. Most companies have many communication strategies. These can include online and offline advertisements, promotional sales, television advertisements, billboards, and more.

In addition to understanding your external market and product-oriented market, you must have a plan in place for your internal growth. This directly supports your marketing efforts, and therefore should be included here. To include this information, you must write about:

- Sales Force: Who will actually be selling your products. You will want to include information such as: how many individuals will be in your sales force, your recruitment and training strategies, ideal compensation plans, and how you will know when to add to your team.
- Sales Activities: These are the strategies your sales force will use to sell. Your sales force will spend its time using these strategies to encourage sales within your company and drive you forward. Some sales-generating activities include making calls, developing customer relationships, selling, turning leads into customers, assisting with reaching sales targets, and more.

It is important to recognize your ideal team as a part of your marketing plan, as your sales force will be a large component of your marketing. Your sales force can build up the reputation of your company and improve your marketing strategies by following through on the promises your marketing strategies make. By focusing on how your sales force will fit into your marketing team, you can ensure that it will always be acting in your company's best interest in mind.

Revenue Model

The section that covers the revenue model will discuss how your company intends to generate revenue. This is an important component of your business plan, as it discusses how you intend to generate revenue and collect capital. Regardless of whether you will be asking for financing, you must complete this section thoroughly. The information you should include in your revenue model is:

- Which revenue source to pursue (how you are going to use your products to generate revenue and which ones).
- What value to offer (the price points you must meet to generate sufficient revenue).

- Who pays for the value (how you will create the value and how you will sell it to ensure you are receiving the value of the product).

Finances

The financial section of your business plan might be a bit broader than the other sections. Here you must include a significant amount of information regarding your current financial position, your historical financial position (if applicable), and where you expect to be in a set amount of time. There are quite a few topics you will need to discuss. Here are the points to include in this section:

- Sales Forecast: Create a spreadsheet and project your sales over the course of a three-year span. You should do a monthly plan for the first year, then a monthly or quarterly plan for the second and third years.
- Expense Budget: You must understand exactly how much it will cost to generate and sell your

products and services. You should include all expenses that will go into starting up your business and being able to offer your product or service. You can have two separate sections: one to express fixed costs (payroll, rent, leases, etc.) and another to express variable costs (advertising, promotions, etc.)

- Cash Flow Statement: This statement will relate the actual money flowing in and out of the business. This should include all variable and fixed costs.
- Income Projections: Using the numbers you placed in your sales forecast, expense budget, and cash flow statements, create an income projection. This will discuss the profits you expect to receive from your business.
- Assets and Liabilities: Have a detailed balance sheet that discusses your assets and liabilities. Start with your assets: cash you have on hand, month-to-month income, inventory (if you have any), and so on. Then include your liabilities, such as debts or other money you

owe. This section can also be called "accounts payable."
- Breakeven Analysis: Include a clear analysis that states at what point you will break even (that is when all your business expenses match your sales volume). You should do this with a three-year projection and ensure that at some point in those three years you will break even.

Unit Economics Overview

Simply put, unit economics refers to the difference in value between direct revenue and the direct costs associated with that revenue acquisition, expressed on a per-unit basis.

You must express how your business will have a positive unit economics because if it has a negative unit economics, you will fail. Essentially, you should express exactly what your unit economics are and how you intend to improve that over the course of business. You should always be working to improve it.

Current Team

Often, people who are inquiring about your business plan will be curious about who you already have in place with your business. It is important to have a section that discusses who your team is. Here, you get the opportunity to showcase who is working for you and what unique and important traits they bring to the table. At this point, you can provide a brief introduction to each member of your current team, as well as provide for each employee an updated resume that expresses his/her exact skills and profile.

Competition

A large part of running a business is recognizing who your competition is and keeping a close eye on them. If you don't know who your competition is, you could get drowned out of your industry. By keeping your eyes on who you're up against, you can stay on-trend, or even better, ahead of the trend. You will also be able to develop a clear account of your strengths and weaknesses and gain other valuable information. When you are discussing your competition, there are a few things you must consider. These include:

- Competitor's Products and Services: Clearly define what products and services your competition offer so that you know exactly how your own products and services compare to theirs. This gives you an opportunity to see where your offering is weak and whether you can make it better so that you are on par with – or, better yet, ahead of – your competition with a cutting-edge, industry-leading product or service. You should also take into consideration the price points at which your competitors offer their products or services, and how these compare with your own.
- Where They Fit in the Market: Knowing where your competitors are in the market compared to you will help significantly when it comes to evaluating your competitors and developing a strategy for staying ahead of the game. This

should include what stage of business they are in, how large their company is, and what their average revenue is. This information helps you understand where you are in relation to your competitors.

- Market Shares: This information allows you to understand how valuable your competitor is in the market.
- Strengths and Weaknesses: In addition to addressing your own strengths and weaknesses, you should pay attention to those of your competition. It can be helpful to understand what their strengths are so that these strengths don't become your weaknesses. Understanding where your competitors' weaknesses lie will also help you develop a strategy in which your strengths offset their weaknesses and give you the competitive edge.
- Importance of Your Audience to Your Competitor: Understanding what level of competition you're in with your competitors will greatly help when it comes to marketing

and market analysis. If your customers are *exactly* the same as your competitors' audiences, you will be in constant direct competition to succeed. However, if your audiences overlap but don't directly compete, you will still have a segment of your market that is easier to attain than those for which you are in direct competition.

- Effect on Your Market Entrance: Consider how your competitors might affect your entrance into the market. Understandably, having a direct competitor that is already established in the market will affect your market entrance. Since they already have loyal customers and you must earn the trust of your new customers, you should expect that this situation could minimize your entrance. Figuring out exactly how this will impact your entrance will help you understand how you can reduce its effects and still have a successful entrance into the market.
- Window of Opportunity: Discover where your window of opportunity is within the market in

comparison to your competitors. What can you provide as a new or refreshed business that they cannot or are not already providing? If you can, provide something they are incapable of providing (or that they simply don't provide), as this will give you a competitive edge and encourage more consumers to consider your product or service.

- Secondary and Indirect Competitors: Make sure you don't get caught up in direct competition. Secondary and indirect competitors can affect your success in the industry, so you must ensure that you are keeping an eye on these competitors as well. Discover why they are secondary or indirect competitors and pay attention to how they could affect your business's success.
- Market Barriers: While other companies can be competition in the market, the market itself can be in competition with your business. Pay attention to any market barriers and how these might affect your business. Market barriers

include such things as evolving technologies, costly investments, etc.

It is crucial that you pay attention to who you are in competition with and where your strengths and weaknesses lie, as well as where your competitors' strengths and weaknesses lie. The clearer you are about your competition, the more you can ensure that your company will have a strong edge when it comes to cutting into the market and becoming successful. If you are not paying attention to your competition, they can easily override you and quickly wash you out of the market. Business is a constantly evolving playing field, and if you are not careful, other companies will recognize your weaknesses and turn them into their own strengths, potentially to the detriment of your own business. By watching your competition, you can learn a lot about your own business.

Historic Investors and Funding

It is important that you share information regarding all historical investors and funding you have received in your business. This information allows others to understand who has already invested in your company and in what amount. If you have ever received investments, you should include all relevant information and documents. When sharing, what amount was invested in your company, you can also take the time to share how you used that investment and what your company was able to do with it. Explain any direct growth that resulted from the investment and any other way it enhanced your company and helped you achieve important business growth.

Having your historical investor and funding information available is especially important if you are requesting funding for your business. Potential and future investors will be interested in knowing what you have already received and whether you were able to use it effectively. They will be curious about your ability to repay the investment and whether you did so in a timely manner. Having this information available and upfront will help potential investors get a clear outline of what their investor relationship with you might look like.

Your Request

If you are requesting funding for your business, you will need a section dedicated to this request. In this section, you must include exactly what you are requesting for your company. There is some important information you will want to include in this section that will help investors understand exactly what you are asking for, as well as why you are asking for it. This section should appear second to last (just before the appendix), as you will want potential investors to know everything about your company before you ask for anything from them. In this section, you will want to include the following information:

- Your Exact Request: Including exactly how much funding you are requesting. Be specific.
- Future Funding Requests: If you are going to require more funding over the next five years, include that here. This will allow your potential investors to learn whether you will be seeking funding in the future and why you are not asking for that funding now. In other words, briefly, explain why you are requesting funding now, and then again later.
- Plans for Funding: When asking for funding, be very clear about what you intend to do with it. Investors will want to know exactly what your intentions are for the money they are giving you. If you are planning to use it for acquisitions, debt retirement, working capital, or anything else, you will need to be clear about that.
- Financial Situational Plans for the Future: If you have any intentions of making significant strategical financial situations for the future, include that information. This would include

anything such as buyouts, debt repayment plans, plans to sell your business or any other major plan that will affect your finances.

In this section, you should focus on what you are asking for now and what you might need in the future. Be upfront. If you are including information about future funding requests, clearly explain why you will need that funding and what you will use it for. Investors might ask why you will be asking for more down the road instead of asking for all of it upfront, so be prepared to answer that question.

Business Plan Appendix

An appendix is not mandatory, but in my professional opinion, every single business plan should have one. Your appendix gives you an opportunity to "ramble" in a structured method. That is, any information you have that supports topics in your business plan but that did not neatly fit into your categories can be cited and explained in this section. You can then discuss each topic in an organized method and share any and all relevant information that did not fit elsewhere. In this section of your business plan, you can include information such as:

- Credit histories (for yourself and your business).
- Resumes for all your company's key managers and the roles they directly play.
- Detailed pictures of your products, including any that portray the uniqueness of your product.
- Any reference letters you may have supporting your request for your company.
- All studies and research details and results you have collected with respect to research you have conducted.
- Any relevant magazine articles or book references you may have used.
- Information regarding your patents, permits, or licenses, even if they are still pending.

- Any and all legal documents you may have used throughout your business plan.
- Copies of all relevant leases.
- Copies of any building permit(s) you hold.
- Copies of all pre-existing contracts pertaining to your business.
- A clear list of all your business consultants, including your accountant and attorney.

Keep track of the number of copies you have made of your business plan and control where they go and who sees them. The information portrayed in this document is important, so it is a good idea to prevent it from reaching your competitors. Finally, you should include a private placement disclaimer at the end of your business plan, especially if you plan to use it in raising capital.

Having a well-structured and thoroughly supported business plan is important for any business. Even if you don't believe that you will be requesting funding anytime soon, having the document already created will allow you to update it if the need arises simply. In addition, the business plan will help you simplify your decision-making processes, meet your entrepreneurial goals, manage your cash flow, and have a clear action plan. It is important that you invest time in making this a quality document that will give you a solid foundation for anything you intend to do with your business in the future. Whether you are looking to partner with others, gain funding, or take serious business action, you will benefit from your business plan.

Chapter 3

Business Plan Example

Learning exactly what you must include in your business plan is helpful, but sometimes it can be even more beneficial to have a clear example of what you must do. In this section, we will review a clear example of what your business plan should look like. This way, you can see exactly how you should be writing your business plan and what it should look like to be a professional and successful document. The better your business plan is, the more likely it will be successful in serving the need you intend it to serve.

In this example, we are going to explore a business plan for Rose Buds Bakery. You will see each section as if it were created for an actual business, understand exactly what information should be provided, and what it should look like. When you are creating your own business plan, you can refer back to this one for an idea of how your own should look. Keep in mind that this example is written for a bakery, so yours might look slightly different. Different business models will have different business plans, but the basics are similar.

Executive Summary

Introduction:

Rose Bud Bakery (RBB) is a start-up cupcake bakery retail establishment located in the heart of Colorado. RBB intends to capture the interest of a regular loyal customer base through its wide variety of gourmet cupcakes and custom-baked goods. Due to the owner's industry experience and mild competition in the area, the company plans to build a strong market in the downtown core.

RBB plans to offer all its products at a competitive price point that will meet the demands of the middle-to-high-income market of local residents and tourists.

The Company:
RBB is a limited partnership incorporation in the state of Colorado. It is owned and managed independently.

Mrs. Althea Rose has a lengthy history in culinary baking, specializing in baking custom cakes and cupcakes. She also brings twenty combined years of experience in finance and administration.

The company plans to hire two full-time cupcake bakers, as well as two part-time cupcake bakers. These employees will work alongside Mrs. Rose to ensure that all baking demands are met, customer service needs are fulfilled, and other day-to-day operations are attended to.

Products and Services

RBB offers a wide variety of cupcake flavors and toppings to produce specialty cupcakes and fulfills custom orders. All ingredients are chosen from American-based producers to ensure maximum freshness and quality. Each cupcake served in the store is baked the same day and carefully detailed by culinary bakers who are at the top of their industry.

In addition to in-store specialties, RBB offers custom products to any individual seeking to feature high-quality, artistic cupcakes or cakes at their event. These cakes are available in any flavor the bakery offers, except for seasonal-based flavors, which will not be offered off-season to maintain the quality of freshness. Thanks to the high-quality training held by the bakers, the cakes and cupcakes can be made to reflect any desired look or design.

Target Market

The baking industry, specifically that part of the industry centered around cupcakes, has experienced rapid growth in recent years. Due to trends in social media and on television, consumers are looking to experience the most unique cupcake ever.

RBB intends to establish a large customer base with strong customer loyalty while still appealing to the rich tourism industry in Colorado. Therefore, RBB will focus its marketing efforts on local residents as well as tourists intending to visit the Colorado area. While local residents will provide a sustainable market base for the company, RBB believes that its biggest success will come from tourists looking to experience unique cupcakes. The company expects that tourism traffic will generate approximately 55% of total revenues. High visibility and unique, attractive products will be key in attracting this important segment of the market.

Target Market Size

The Colorado tourism industry saw 77.7 million visitors in the year 2015, up 7% from a year before. Those tourists spent a total of $19.1 billion in the state of Colorado. Because of this, the company aims to see approximately 500,000 visitors in its first year of business. These visitors will be a combination of tourists and local residents who are eager to see the unique baked goods that RBB offers.

Market Plan

RBB wants to target the market by having a high-visibility location effectively. Also, the company plans to place advertisements in the local area on strategically, but not limited to, billboards, transit stops, signage, and more. These targeted advertisements will attract consumers already in Colorado.

Online marketing strategies will also be secured to attract incoming tourists and ensure they add RBB to their itinerary. A website will be created so that potential consumers can get a feel for the company and what the experience has to offer. To target the online market, social media advertisements, pay-per-click advertisements, and online influencers will be paid monthly. This will encourage incoming tourists to visit our location and experience our specialty cupcakes.

Revenue Model

RBB intends to collect revenue from the sale of specialty cupcakes and custom orders. The specialty cupcakes will be valued between $3-$5 each, depending on the intricacy of detailing. The specialty cakes will range between $150-$750, also dependent upon the amount of detail involved in designing the cake. Sales of cupcakes will be made to tourists and local residents, while sales of custom orders will be made to those hosting events in the local area.

Finances

The following charts, graphs, and statements reflect the financial projections of RBB in the company's first year of business.

Sales Forecast

The following charts reflect the projected sales to be made in the first three years of business. These charts reflect conservative, moderate, and optimistic market climates to ensure all potential conditions are considered.

Year One, Months 1 through 12

Month	Conservative Sales	Moderate Sales	Optimistic Sales
1 Jan.	$4750 (475 specialty) $8125 (25 custom) =$12,875	$5220 (522 specialty) $8775 (27 custom) =$13,995	$5740 (574 specialty) $9750 (30 custom) =$15,490
2 Feb.	$4750 (475 specialty) $8125 (25 custom) =$12,875	$5220 (522 specialty) $8775 (27 custom) =$13,995	$5740 (574 specialty) $9750 (30 custom) =$15,490
3 Mar.	$4500 (450 specialty) $6500 (18 custom) =$11,000	$4950 (495 specialty) $6175 (19 custom) =$11,125	$5440 (544 specialty) $6825 (21 custom) =$12,265
4 Apr.	$4500 (450 specialty) $6500 (18 custom) =$11,000	$4950 (495 specialty) $6175 (19 custom) =$11,125	$5440 (544 specialty) $6825 (21 custom) =$12,265
5 May	$4500 (450 specialty) $6500 (18 custom) =$11,000	$4950 (495 specialty) $6175 (19 custom) =$11,125	$5440 (544 specialty) $6825 (21 custom) =$12,265
6 Jun.	$4750 (475 specialty) $8125 (25 custom) =$12,875	$5220 (522 specialty) $8775 (27 custom) =$13,995	$5740 (574 specialty) $9750 (30 custom) =$15,490
7 Jul.	$4750 (475 specialty) $8125	$5220 (522 specialty) $8775	$5740 (574 specialty) $9750

	(25 custom) =$12,875	(27 custom) =$13,995	(30 custom) =$15,490
8 Aug.	$4750 (475 specialty) $8125 (25 custom) =$12,875	$5220 (522 specialty) $8775 (27 custom) =$13,995	$5740 (574 specialty) $9750 (30 custom) =$15,490
9 Sept.	$4500 (450 specialty) $6500 (18 custom) =$11,000	$4950 (495 specialty) $6175 (19 custom) =$11,125	$5440 (544 specialty) $6825 (21 custom) =$12,265
10 Oct.	$4500 (450 specialty) $6500 (18 custom) =$11,000	$4950 (495 specialty) $6175 (19 custom) =$11,125	$5440 (544 specialty) $6825 (21 custom) =$12,265
11 Nov.	$4750 (475 specialty) $8125 (25 custom) =$12,875	$5220 (522 specialty) $8775 (27 custom) =$13,995	$5740 (574 specialty) $9750 (30 custom) =$15,490
12 Dec.	$4750 (475 specialty) $8125 (25 custom) =$12,875	$5220 (522 specialty) $8775 (27 custom) =$13,995	$5740 (574 specialty) $9750 (30 custom) =$15,490

Year Two and Three, Quarterly

Quarter	Conservative	Moderate	Optimistic
Year Two/Q1	$40,425	$43,026	$47,569
Year Two/Q2	$38,362	$39,869	$44,022
Year Two/Q3	$40,425	$43,026	$47,569
Year Two/Q4	$40,425	$43,026	$47,569
Year Three/Q1	$44,467	$47,328	$52,325
Year Three/Q2	$42,198	$43,855	$48,424
Year Three/Q3	$44,467	$47,328	$52,325
Year Three/Q4	$44,467	$47,328	$52,325

Expense Budget

The following charts reflect the projected expense budget for the next three years. In year one, RBB has expressed the expenses per month. In years two and three, it has expressed the expenses in quarterly periods.

Year One, Monthly

Month	Fixed Expenses	Cost	Variable Expenses	Cost	Total
1	Rent Utilities Payroll Business Insurance Banking Fees	$1200 $300 $7680 $125 $30	Ingredients Equipment Advertising Promotions	$750 $500 $500 $250	$11,335
2	Rent Utilities Payroll Business Insurance Banking Fees	$1200 $300 $7680 $125 $30	Ingredients Equipment Advertising Promotions	$750 $500 $500 $250	$11,335
3	Rent Utilities Payroll Business Insurance Banking Fees	$1200 $300 $7680 $125 $30	Ingredients Equipment Advertising Promotions	$600 $300 $350 $100	$10,685
4	Rent Utilities Payroll Business Insurance Banking Fees	$1200 $300 $7680 $125 $30	Ingredients Equipment Advertising Promotions	$600 $300 $350 $100	$10,685
5	Rent Utilities Payroll Business Insurance	$1200 $300 $7680 $125 $30	Ingredients Equipment Advertising Promotions	$600 $300 $350 $100	$10,685

	Banking Fees				
6	Rent Utilities Payroll Business Insurance Banking Fees	$1200 $300 $7680 $125 $30	Ingredients Equipment Advertising Promotions	$750 $500 $500 $250	$11,335
7	Rent Utilities Payroll Business Insurance Banking Fees	$1200 $300 $7680 $125 $30	Ingredients Equipment Advertising Promotions	$750 $500 $500 $250	$11,335
8	Rent Utilities Payroll Business Insurance Banking Fees	$1200 $300 $7680 $125 $30	Ingredients Equipment Advertising Promotions	$750 $500 $500 $250	$11,335
9	Rent Utilities Payroll Business Insurance Banking Fees	$1200 $300 $7680 $125 $30	Ingredients Equipment Advertising Promotions	$600 $300 $350 $100	$10,685
10	Rent Utilities Payroll Business Insurance Banking Fees	$1200 $300 $7680 $125 $30	Ingredients Equipment Advertising Promotions	$600 $300 $350 $100	$10,685

11	Rent Utilities Payroll Business Insurance Banking Fees	$1200 $300 $7680 $125 $30	Ingredients Equipment Advertising Promotions	$750 $500 $500 $250	$11,335
12	Rent Utilities Payroll Business Insurance Banking Fees	$1200 $300 $7680 $125 $30	Ingredients Equipment Advertising Promotions	$750 $500 $500 $250	$11,335

Years Two and Three, Quarterly

Quarter	Fixed Expenses	Cost	Variable Expenses	Cost	Total
Year 2/Q1	Rent Utilities Payroll Business Insurance Banking Fees	$3600 $900 $23,040 $425 $90	Ingredients Equipment Advertising Promotions	$2310 $1430 $1485 $660	$33,940
Year 2/Q2	Rent Utilities Payroll Business Insurance Banking Fees	$3600 $900 $23,040 $425 $90	Ingredients Equipment Advertising Promotions	$1950 $1100 $1200 $450	$32,755
Year 2/Q3	Rent Utilities Payroll Business Insurance Banking Fees	$3600 $900 $23,040 $425 $90	Ingredients Equipment Advertising Promotions	$2310 $1430 $1485 $660	$33,940
Year 2/Q4	Rent Utilities Payroll Business Insurance Banking Fees	$3600 $900 $23,040 $425 $90	Ingredients Equipment Advertising Promotions	$2310 $1430 $1485 $660	$33,940
Year 3/Q1	Rent Utilities Payroll Business Insurance Banking Fees	$3600 $900 $23,040 $425 $90	Ingredients Equipment Advertising Promotions	$2541 $1573 $1633 $726	$34,528
Year 3/Q2	Rent Utilities Payroll	$3600 $900 $23,040	Ingredients Equipment Advertising	$2145 $1210 $1320	$33,225

	Business Insurance Banking Fees	$425 $90	Promotions	$495	
Year 3/Q3	Rent Utilities Payroll Business Insurance Banking Fees	$3600 $900 $23,040 $425 $90	Ingredients Equipment Advertising Promotions	$2541 $1573 $1633 $726	$34,528
Year 3/Q4	Rent Utilities Payroll Business Insurance Banking Fees	$3600 $900 $23,040 $425 $90	Ingredients Equipment Advertising Promotions	$2541 $1573 $1633 $726	$34,528

Cash Flow Statement

The following charts reflect the cash flow RBB expects to see in years one through three. Year one is charted first, reflecting the monthly cash flow projections. Years two and three, respectively, are charted second, reflecting quarterly cash flow projections.

Year One, Monthly

Month	Incoming*	Outgoing
1	$14,120	$11,335
2	$14,120	$11,335
3	$11,463	$10,685
4	$11,463	$10,685
5	$11,463	$10,685
6	$14,120	$11,335
7	$14,120	$11,335
8	$14,120	$11,335
9	$11,463	$10,685
10	$11,463	$10,685
11	$14,120	$11,335
12	$14,120	$11,335

*Incoming number is the *average* amount of incoming capital. This *average number* has been calculated by adding the conservative, moderate, and optimistic sales forecast projections and dividing them by three.

Years Two and Three, Quarterly

Quarter	Incoming*	Outgoing
Year 2/Q1	$43,673	$33,940
Year 2/Q2	$40,751	$32,755
Year 2/Q3	$43,673	$33,940
Year 2/Q4	$43,673	$33,940
Year 3/Q1	$48,040	$34,528
Year 3/Q2	$44,825	$33,225
Year 3/Q3	$48,040	$34,528
Year 3/Q4	$48,040	$34,528

*Incoming number is the *average* amount of incoming capital. This *average number* has been calculated by adding the conservative, moderate, and optimistic sales forecast projections and dividing them by three.

Income Projection

The following chart displays RBB's projected income for years one, two, and three, respectively. These projections are displayed on an annual basis.

	Year 1	Year 2	Year 3
Income Projection	+$23,385	+$37,195	+$52,136

Assets and Liabilities

The following chart conveys RBB's assets and liabilities.

Assets	Liabilities
Specialty Convection Oven $10,000	Store Front $55,000
Cash on Hand $25,000	Business Loan $25,000
Month-to-Month Income $13,000	Delivery Vehicle $20,000
Inventory $7000	
$55,000	$100,000

Breakeven Analysis

Based on the financial analysis for RBB, the company projects it will break even in quarter three of year two. At this time, the business will be out of debt and running for-profit.

Unit Economics Overview

The following chart expresses the unit economics overview for RBB. This business portrays the cost to open the business. Month-to-month costs can be reviewed in the finances section of the business plan.

Cost to Open Business

Building Lease	$55,000
Business Loan	$25,000
Equipment	$20,000
Staff	$7680
Insurances	$1300
Permits and Business Licenses	$1500
Website	$3000
Delivery Vehicle	$20,000
Total	$133,000

Current Team

RBB is currently operated as a sole proprietorship by Althea Rose. Mrs. Rose has a degree in Culinary Baking and also possesses 20 combined years of business experience in areas including accounting, administrations, and management.

The company intends to hire an additional four bakers – two part-time and two full-time – prior to the grand opening. They will be trained for one month beforehand to ensure they are prepared to handle the demands of the bakery alongside Mrs. Rose.

Competition

While the Colorado area has a significant number of bakeries, none are dedicated to specialty cake designs. There will be some competition in the form of baked goods; however, RBB does not expect to experience any direct competition when it comes to custom cakes. In addition, the bakers in the vicinity are not trained in culinary bakery, and therefore do not hold the same qualifications that Mrs. Rose does and that her staff will.

It is expected that the uniqueness of the bakery and the specialty of the cakes will encourage visitors to choose RBB over another bakery in the local area. While there may be resistance in encouraging loyal customers of surrounding bakeries to choose RBB instead, the company believes that the exclusivity of its products will encourage customers to shop.

The surrounding competition does maintain the strength of having a wider variety of options available to customers, with various pastries and cakes available. However, none have the range of flavors and expertise baked into the cakes that RBB will. Because of this, RBB believes it will be able to develop a loyal customer following as well as encourage out-of-town tourists to visit the bakery due to its unique and welcoming appearance and offers.

Also, only three bakeries in the state offer the type of high-quality custom cakes that RBB will offer. These bakeries are each more than 30 miles away, meaning RBB will not have any direct competition in the immediate area.

Historic Investors and Funding

RBB has requested and been approved for one $25,000 business loan and one $20,000 car loan. These loans are outstanding, with a remaining combined balance of $43,000 due.

Request

RBB requests a $75,000 loan with a promise to repay and an offering of 20% of the business ownership in return. This loan will be used to assist in incorporating the company, entering a storefront, and purchasing all necessary equipment to operate a new bakery. In addition, the company intends to pay back the $43,000 remaining balances with this loan. The remainder of the loan will be used to hire and train new staff, promote the store, and acquire new inventory.

RBB intends to repay this loan over a seven-year period. At the end of the seven-year period, RBB requests the opportunity to purchase back the 20% ownership.

Chapter 4

Common Mistakes to Avoid

While a business plan might seem easy to create, many common mistakes are often made. Because a business plan is a professional document, it is crucial that you avoid these common mistakes, which can invalidate any requests you intend to make with the business plan. Below we are going to explore some of the most common mistakes made by individuals who are writing a business plan.

Poor Writing Skills

Not everyone is an amazing writer, and that is OK. If you are one of these people, it's a good idea to hire someone to write your business plan with you. A business plan littered with poor grammar, spelling errors and incorrect punctuation will diminish the quality of your business plan. Investors don't expect you to be an English major, but they do expect you to have a professional document that is written...well...professionally. A document that does not reflect professionalism will lead investors to believe that you are not going to be professional in other areas, which could lead to a lack of investments.

Professional Presentation

Although it may not seem important to you, it is important to investors that your business plan *looks* good. That means your margins, labels, headings, and other important elements of the document are uniform and in an easy-to-read font. Additionally, no pages should be missing, graphs should be presented properly with the units correctly chosen and displayed, technical terminology should be defined, and a table of contents should be included.

It is important that you have someone else proofread your presentation. This will help with grammar, punctuation, and spelling, and ensure that your document looks professional. You should also double-check to make sure everything is in there and in the correct place. It is better to learn in advance that something is missing than to find out it is missing only when an important investor is looking over your document.

Incompletion

Some individuals create a plan but don't research it extensively enough or ensure that it includes everything necessary for investors to consider. If you are nearing the completion of your business plan, ensure that you included as much information as possible and that every section was thoroughly discussed. This will ensure that investors have all the information they need to make a decision, hopefully in your favor.

Vague Planning

Investors want to see specifics. Before they hand over a significant amount of money for you to design your business, they want to ensure that you actually have a plan to design your business. Investors do not want to invest first and watch you plan later. If they were to do this, the chances would be significantly higher that they would be investing in businesses that were not legit and they would be out several hundreds of thousands of dollars. Instead, they want to know that if they are investing in you, you have a strong business plan and a clear direction. They also want to ensure that you (and they) know exactly what you are doing with your business, how you intend to use the money they invest in you, and how you intend to create the money to pay them back.

Excessive Details

Although you might think the more, the better, some people get too caught up in details and include way more information than investors care to know. If this is the case, investors will become confused and won't want to sift through all the information you have provided to figure out exactly what your business is and why you are asking for money. Make sure you stay *extremely* focused in the correct headings. If you have extra information that you feel is relevant to the business plan, first make sure it doesn't fit *perfectly* under any existing headings. If it doesn't, add it to the appendix.

Unrealistic or Unfounded Assumptions

This is where it becomes important that you adequately research your business, including your target market, sales projections, and anything else related to the success of your business. If investors believe that your projections or assumptions are unfounded or unrealistic, they will not invest in you. This raises a big red flag, as it leads them to believe that you are incapable of effectively researching your market or that you don't actually know who (or how big) your target market is. In this case, investors will not want to invest in you because you cannot actually guarantee that you will be able to repay the investment.

Inadequate Research

It is important that your facts are actually factual and that you draw research from reliable sources. It is also important that your information is accurate. Investors hear about various industries, and often keep tabs on their preferred industries as well. This means they will know if you are making assumptions that are not fact-based. If you have not conducted enough research, an investor will be able to tell. Additionally, if you have not conducted enough research and for some reason, it slides through, and you *do* get an investment, you may be left high and dry if your assumptions were incorrect and you do not perform as well as you expected. This is almost worse than not getting the investment in the first place, as now you are out a business *and* whatever your requested investment was.

"No Risk" Claims

The second you say "no risk," an investor stops listening. There is no such thing as "no risk, " and this claim will make you seem unfit to be a business owner. Investors know there is a risk; if you don't know this, you raise a red flag that you may not take the investment or business seriously. If you make this claim, there is a good chance that investors will immediately stop listening to you and will definitely not give you money.

"No Competition" Claims

Many businesses will say they have "no competition." Much like the "no risk" claim, this instantly raises a red flag with investors. The reality is, no matter what market you're in, you have competition. Many companies fail to truly research their competition or the secondary or indirect competition their businesses are up against. If you claim you have "no competition," your investor will likely ask you to research deeper and may deny an investment altogether.

Your Business "Plan" is a Business "Idea"

A business plan should say how you intend to get from one stage to the next: short-term, mid-term, and long-term. If your business plan merely states the stages of business at each point and fails to explain how you will get to each stage, you will not get investors. Investors want to ensure that you are actually considering *how* you will get from one stage to the next. They must make sure a viable action plan exists for your business to grow and ultimately for you to pay back your loan. You must make sure your plan is a plan and not merely an overview of the various stages of your business.

Ways to Avoid Common Mistakes

Now that you have seen some of the most common mistakes, you are probably wondering how to avoid them. Writing a business plan is a lengthy process, and it is better to do it right the first time as opposed to restructuring or redoing it several times over. By ensuring you get your business plan right the first time, you can avoid making any of the common mistakes listed above. Many of these mistakes can be fatal to your company's ability to receive funding or support, so it is important that you do not include them in your document. Following is a list of ways you can get your business plan right the first time to avoid making any of these major mistakes.

Evaluating New Business Ideas

Many new business startups fail to evaluate the quality of their business ideas. The reality is, not every idea is going to be as great as we think it will be. There are a few reasons why a business might not be a good idea, including: it is too costly an investment/there is not enough return, it will not break even, there is not enough demand in the market and more. To prevent this issue from developing in your own business, you must evaluate every new business idea you develop. Ideally, you should do this *before* you begin the time-consuming process of developing a business idea. However, if you are working on a business plan and hit the finances section, then realize a chance exists that your business won't break even or won't become profitable, you will likely need to reevaluate the business idea altogether.

There are a few ways to evaluate a business idea. These include:

- Create a rough draft of your breakeven analysis and see if your company will become profitable within three years.
- Identify whether a big enough need exists for the product or service you intend to offer.
- Figure out if your business is different enough from existing offers in the market to ensure you will not be disregarded for an existing establishment.
- Understand what your market size is. Even if there is a strong need for your product or service, your business won't necessarily have enough long-lasting customers to make it worthwhile.

- Determine the cost to begin your business. Is it going to be expensive? If there are ways to reduce the budget, are they going to cost you productivity and profits in the future? Will you be able to find a way to afford startup costs? If expenses are too high, it might not be worth it.

Conduct Effective Research

Ideally, you have already done some research for your business evaluation. However, when you are writing a business plan, you must go deeper than the surface. The more extensive your research is on the specific topics relating to your business, the better you will be able to plan your business moves. This way, you can ensure that you have thoroughly reviewed all potential situations and marked a clear path from point A to point B. If you do not research enough, you might find that you have a hard time making a business action plan because you do not know exactly what is involved in making it work. You must conduct effective research when it comes to your market, your target audience, your budget, and anything else associated with your business plan. Ideally, you should invest significant time in researching your market audience, as these are the individuals you are looking to serve; the more knowledge about them you have, the easier it will be to serve them.

Research Competitors

In addition to conducting extensive research on your own business, you must conduct research on your competition. Beyond knowing who your competition is, it can be beneficial to research what your competition has done in the past and how it has (or hasn't) worked. This information will help you steer clear of acts that are not effective and will guide you to strategies that work. Because your competition is already established, there is a good chance that you can learn a great deal from them. The more you know, the more you can identify their strengths and weaknesses. Then you can brace yourself against their strengths and accentuate your business to offset their weaknesses. This will help you enter the market as a feasible competitor.

In addition to the advantage this knowledge can give you, it also helps you greatly when it comes to getting potential investors. When you are approaching investors with your presentation, they are going to want to know exactly who your competition is, why they are your competition, and how you plan to compete with them. Because you are a startup, they will realize that you have a disadvantage, as your competition already has a loyal customer base. This means you will need to spend time discovering how you can use your marketing strategies, products, and/or services to build your own loyal customer following.

Feedback Is Important!

Gaining feedback about your business plan, as well as about your products and/or services, is a great opportunity to see what people actually think and where you can improve. You can solicit feedback about these areas in various ways depending on whom you are trying to gain feedback from.

When seeking feedback about your business plan, you can hire a professional to proofread it or simply have another professional who is familiar with business plans look it over. At this point, he/she can offer feedback regarding where you might consider fixing the business plan, whether its appearance is right, and whether it is a strong leveraging device for gaining investors. This is incredibly important to do at the end of your business planning because one set of eyes isn't always enough to catch common mistakes that could be detrimental to your presentations.

Alternatively, you should focus on gaining feedback throughout the duration of your business evaluation and business plan research efforts. Gaining feedback from potential customers and anyone else involved in the product or service, such as manufacturers, sales teams, or otherwise, is vital to your success. This gives you an opportunity to see where your product meets the market's needs and where you can improve. You can perfect your product the first time instead of having it reach the market and then realize that it was not as great as it could have been had you taken the time to implement this step. You can gain feedback through surveys or by giving out a limited number of prototypes to select individuals who can physically test the product or service and give you direct feedback. This is often called a "beta test" and is commonly used for many products and services. It is a great tool and highly recommended for use!

Hire a Professional

Not everyone will have an easy time writing a business plan. For some, spelling and grammar, research, and other important elements of the business plan can be very difficult. If this rings true for you, don't fret! A great idea is to use this book as an opportunity to create the foundation of your business plan, then hire a professional to help you do the rest. That way, you can reduce costs by having done most of the work yourself and hiring a professional only to complete the bits with which you are having difficulty. There are many professionals out there who are incredibly talented when it comes to creating effective business plans. They will be able to work alongside you to take your vision and capture it on paper, creating an award-winning presentation that should land any investor's interest.

Chapter 5

Choosing a Niche

The word "niche" is very popular in the business world. A niche is a great opportunity to focus on a specific area of the market to achieve higher quality results. If you haven't already, you should consider choosing a niche. Creating a business plan without a niche can lead you to quickly realize that you will require *a lot* of capital to market to the various individuals in your target industry effectively, or that you will fail. Choosing a niche is a great opportunity to reduce the size of your audience and make your efforts more effective. In this chapter, you will learn exactly how you can choose a niche.

What is a Niche?

Simply put, a niche is a small segment of the market that is interested in specialized products. Essentially, a niche is a smaller portion of your target market that will be interested specifically in your products. It is a specific demographic and psychographic of customers who have a set of needs you will fulfill with your product or service. Unlike the rest of the market, a niche will stand out in a certain way and will be drawn to your company to fulfill its common need. The rest of the market will not have this specific need, and therefore your business will not be considered relevant to them.

Why Do I Need One?

With industry markets often boasting millions, sometimes billions, of customers, it's clear that you won't be able to reach every single niche in your industry's market, especially if you're a startup. The cost would be astronomical and likely more than an investor would be willing to pay. Narrowing down to a niche allows you to focus on a specific set of consumers and fulfill their needs.

Billion-dollar companies, such as major department stores, often have millions to invest in advertising and product and service development.

Because of this, they can satisfy a number of niches with a single business. However, smaller businesses and startups cannot create this type of impact in the market. Therefore, narrowing down your niche allows you to focus specifically on those who will benefit most from your product or service. That way, you can identify exactly who these people are, what their exact need is, how you can alter your product or service to fulfill it, and how to actually reach these people, so they discover your business. If you lack this, you will be, as they say, "shouting to a room full of people who aren't listening." However, if you do have a niche, you will be speaking directly to those who are interested and who want to hear what you have to say (or sell).

In addition to being able to identify and serve the niche market, there are other benefits to having a niche. You can create your entire brand and business "mood" based on your niche's interests. You can also be branded the "expert" in your niche, which will drive even more consumers to your company. The more focused your business is in a specific niche, the more likely you will succeed, especially as a startup or small company.

How Do I Choose One?

It might seem difficult to choose a niche. Many products or services can appeal to a large segment of the market. However, it is not effective to do this. With that in mind, there are several things you will need to consider when buckling down and identifying your niche.

Initially, you will want to identify what needs you personally can fulfill. Since you are the one going into business, it is a good idea to choose a need with which you have experience. For example, a life coach may consider becoming a life coach specifically to new moms because this allows her to speak expertly on an experience about which she knows a lot. Alternatively, a baker may consider selling only pastries because this is the product he/she can create the best. Before you decide on your niche, identify your own strengths and how they may benefit a niche market. You likely have a few, so take your time and write them down. Later, you can identify which one you will choose.

After you have brainstormed a few ideas, figure out which you feel most excited about. Put a star near or highlight the niches about which you feel most passionate, as these are the ones you will want to focus on most. The reality is, you are going to work best in a niche that speaks to you. Therefore, ensure you aren't choosing something just because the research and numbers say it will be the most successful. If you choose an area about which you are not passionate, you will not invest the time or energy necessary to make your business succeed in that industry.

Now that you are clear on what you want to do, you must clarify what is actually needed in the market. There are several ways to do this, including gaining feedback and talking to people within the niche's unique audience. You can start by putting surveys on the internet and directing them to the correct people. Then, you can get on the phone and start speaking with potential clients from each industry. This will allow you to find out exactly what they need and how they would prefer to be served. Finally, you should talk to industry experts and ask for their opinion on each niche. Some things you will want to consider include:

- Which niche has a large enough following to be viable?
- Which niche is growing and which is not?
- How are many businesses (approximately) already fulfilling the niche's needs?
- Would you, as a startup or growing business, be able to compete?

After having phone conversations with industry experts and potential consumers, you can put all your information together and start evaluating which business venture is going to be most successful. You want to make sure the niche you pick will be successful, and also that you are going to feel confident in being a part of that niche. You don't want to choose something that is meaningless to you solely because it could be the most successful. You won't be able to make it a success if you aren't passionate about it, so it is important that you not hop on the bandwagon just to make a quick buck. The best brands and companies are passionate about what they are doing, and that is what keeps them in business for years to come. However, you also don't want to make a decision based solely on passion, then realize there is no market for your product. You will need a balanced option that will be a viable business plan.

Anything Else I Need to Know?

Choosing a niche is, essentially, mandatory. If you are going to open your business successfully, you must choose a niche. It might seem difficult or counterintuitive but choosing a niche is a major factor in having a successful business. Above we indicated some things to consider; however, we know that sometimes it can be more effective to have an actual list of questions to answer. With that in mind, in this section, we have included a list of questions you can think about when you are choosing your business niche.

1. Is there a significant demand for the product?
2. How are the reviews on existing products? What value can you gain from them? (Are sales actually occurring? Are ratings high or low? For low ratings, what caused them and can you effectively change that in your own product or service?)
3. Are you able to create a higher quality version of the product without having the price point set too high?
4. Do the niche and product offer good profit margins?

5. Are the customers in the niche passionate about the product or do they have a strong need for it?
6. Is it easy to find groups of people who are passionate about it?
7. Is the target demographic solid and consistent?
8. Can you create content based around this niche? (E.g., for garden tools you can offer videos with tips and information. For printer ink, you cannot.)
9. Does the potential exist to add consumable products to your business down the line?
10. Is the product availability and/or interest seasonal or can you sell it all year long?
11. Is the product timeless, or will you need to continually update your product line every season/year?
12. Can you offer something unusual or unique that other businesses likely won't offer?
13. Will you be able to add higher priced items later and still receive good sales numbers?

14. Do the customers already own something similar that may prevent them from purchasing?
15. Can you add digital products to your sales later? (e.g., e-books, audio/visual items, etc.)

If you can answer these questions and the answers are in your favor, you have likely chosen a good niche to pursue. Having a good niche that positively answers all the above questions is important because it allows you to build and expand your business with the knowledge that there will be room for you to enter the market and succeed. It also means you will be able to expand your sales, offer future products, and continue to grow your business.

Most Common Mistake When Choosing a Niche

Several common mistakes are made when individuals choose niches for their business. These mistakes are easy to avoid, but if you don't avoid them, they could destroy your company's success. It is important to choose a niche that will be effective for you and your business, so you don't end up running a business that is doomed from the start. The following are reasons why niches are ineffective for certain businesses, or mistakes that businesses make when choosing a niche.

The Niche Isn't Big Enough

A very common mistake people make when choosing a niche is choosing one that is *too* focused. While you want to have a niche small enough that your company can appeal to it, you don't want your niche to be too small. Having a niche that is too small can result in your not having enough customers to keep your business going. Not everyone in your niche will buy your products or services, and once the others do, you will not have a market to cater to anymore.

The Niche Isn't Growing

Another common mistake people overlook is choosing a niche that isn't growing. While having a niche is important, it's also important to research that niche just as you would your target audience. Because, well, it *is* your target audience! You must ensure the niche is growing and that it will continue growing for the foreseeable future. A niche that is not growing, or that is growing too slow, won't leave much room for expansion in your business. If you intend to choose a good one, make sure you choose a niche that is growing at a healthy rate. Additionally, make sure you can satisfy the needs of that niche with your products and services.

You're Not Passionate About the Niche

It really doesn't matter how incredible your niche is if you are not passionate or even remotely interested in it. Having a niche is important because it gives you a narrower focus, but if you choose one because you feel that it has more to offer than the one about which you're actually passionate, you will almost definitely fail. This is because we tend to work less at something we are not passionate about because the results don't bring us joy. The idea of lots of money is nice, but if we don't enjoy making it, we will quickly become run down and no longer want to work in the business. The entire point of becoming an entrepreneur is to command your own time and finances, so you want to ensure you are doing something that will make you happy and about which you will be passionate. This is why you were prompted to highlight those niches you were most interested in or, better yet, most passionate about in the "choose your niche" section. Understanding what you are *most* interested in will help you choose your niche and commit to it. Even if the conditions are not as ideal as the optimal niche, as long as they aren't "doomed," you should be good to go! The idea is to pick a niche that will offer you enough business to keep running; it doesn't have to be the best possible niche in the entire market.

The more passionate you are, the easier it will be to reach your business goals. Also, it is a lot easier to be labeled the niche's "expert" if you are actually passionate about it because you will want to know more and you will be excited about sharing it. Consumers gravitate towards those who are passionate and excited about their businesses, which gives you a great advantage with your company!

You're Not Knowledgeable About the Niche
It is important that you spend time understanding the niche and its needs. Just because you feel that you can serve a niche well doesn't mean you are equipped to do so. You can certainly develop the knowledge necessary to serve the niche effectively but if you don't do this beforehand, you could fail miserably. It is important to put in the time and research before launching your business, or new products and services so that you can be certain you are clear on what the niche is all about. You should be knowledgeable in many areas

surrounding your niche. These areas include who your customers are, what they want, what they like, what your product or service is, what your product or service does, why your product or service is desirable, and how you can grow the idea in the future to continually grow your business. The better you understand your niche, the easier it will be to build an empire within it. If you are unclear about who you are targeting or what they need, you are not going to be able to get your products or services into the hands of those who would otherwise be interested in them. Additionally, if you are not clear about your product or service, you will not know how to construct one that will attract your target audience and keep them coming back. You must be equipped to understand everything, including how you can expand your existing offers so that you can continually build a great company. No company has stayed in business off a single static product or service. Business requires change and growth. Consumer interests and habits will change, so your business must be prepared to keep up.

You Have Insufficient Interest in the Product or Service

Another issue people have is that they are clear on their niche and its needs but fail to make a product or service that effectively meets those needs. Generally, this happens when the need or want is not strong enough, or when the company did not have enough information on how to fulfill said need. If this happens, you could end up investing a significant amount of time and money into developing something that no one will buy. It is important to make sure you spend a great deal of time and energy in your investigating stages. It may seem like it isn't worth your while because it takes so long, but the reality is that the more time you spend preparing, the easier it will be for your business to succeed in the long run. If you have specifically chosen your target audience, if you are marketing to them, and if it "should" be effective but your efforts are not returning any quality results, it is time to evaluate your product and service again. Doing this will allow you to look at anything that may be wrong or to determine why your target audience is not accepting your product/service. Some questions you might consider asking yourself or your team include:

- Is the price point fair?
- Does it compete well with similar products?
- Is the product of high enough quality for your customers?
- Is the product attractive enough for your customers?
- Does it effectively fulfill a need or want in the market?
- Is there a high need for this product or service?

Asking the above questions will help you pinpoint what is wrong with your product or service and assist you in making the necessary changes. Once you reevaluate this section, you can reconstruct your product or service and relaunch it to the market. Companies that do this generally label the product "2.0" or include a name in the title that expresses the fact that it is new and improved. This will allow you to start from scratch and hopefully do better with your sales in the future. If there are too many things wrong with your product, however, it may be best to scrap it and start planning a new product or service that can fulfill your target audience's needs.

You Have Too Many Niches

You might feel compelled to choose a couple of niches. Perhaps you feel that this will expand your reach or increase your sales opportunities. The reality is, this widens your audience too much and makes it nearly impossible to cater to everyone. Different segments of your market require different types of communication, interaction, sales strategies, and even products and services. If you absolutely feel that you must go with two niches, build each with its own structure and make sure you market each separately, including unique advertisements, websites, etc. The more you try to combine the niches, the more confusing your efforts will become and the less effective you will be at reaching anyone who might benefit from your products or services.

You Fail to Effectively Market to your Niche
After choosing a niche, many people fail to understand how they can actually interact with it. Just because you are speaking to a specific group of people doesn't mean they're listening. To make sure you are effectively reaching your niche, you must invest more in your research. It always goes back to effectively researching the market. If you have a clear understanding of who you are talking to, you will be able to customize all your efforts to satisfy this group of people. That includes understanding how to market to them, how to speak to them, what age of employees they prefer to work with, what products or services actually fulfill their needs and wants, and more. You must

understand all this important and basic information if you are going to sell to your target audience effectively. Without understanding, you might end up marketing with language and stories – or even colors and pictures – that don't appeal to those whom you are trying to sell to. If this is the case, you will find that your marketing efforts will fail because they will not compel your intended audience to do anything; this is because your intended audience will not even be paying attention.

You Cannot Create New Products/Consumables
Business requires you to release new things for consumers to purchase continually. Every product and service have its lifecycle, including an end of its life expectancy. No product is so timeless that it doesn't require an upgrade. It is important that you choose a product or service that will allow you to expand on your existing line and offer more in the future. Many businesses rely on the sale of consumables or other items that encourage

existing customers to return to purchase other products. For example, having your own unique watch company with bands that can be interchanged allows consumers to purchase the watch and then return to purchase new bands for the watch. It is important to ensure that the product you have chosen will allow you to develop a customer base that you can nurture through the release of future products. Doing this will allow you to stay in business for years and to continue selling and growing your business.

You Experience Difficulties with Content Creation

A major mistake many individuals make, especially those just going into business, is choosing a niche that does not have the opportunity to create ongoing content. These days, an online presence is a major part of being able to sell your products. An online presence relies heavily on the existence of content creation, which ultimately means you must be able to produce content on a regular basis, including blogs posts or videos with advice on how to get the most out of the products or other information that nurtures the niche. For example, a pet store might have a blog that is consistently updated with interesting facts about the types of pets they cater to, as well as news about the pet industry or relevant animals. Doing this allows the store to reach out on the internet constantly, encourages customers to read what the store is talking about, and ultimately develops a relationship with the customers. This type of relationship leads to the creation of loyal customers who will continue to choose your company over any of your competition. If you cannot create quality content for your niche, it may not be a good niche to get into.

Business Plan Template

Business Plan Template

This business plan template is created for a retail store business, though yours should look fairly similar. Adjust the appropriate areas to reflect your particular business model.

Executive Summary

Include specific information about your company: who are you and your partners, where is your business located, when were you established, what do you offer, etc.

Products and Services

Introduce your products and services. Why are they unique, how do you present them, what do you offer, etc.

Target Market

Who is your target market? What industry are you in, what size is it, yearly revenue of the industry, etc.

Target Market Size

How large is the industry? What are the annual growth rates? How much of this industry do you believe you can reach and serve?

Market Plan

How do you intend to reach your target audience and market to them? What strategies do you intend to use? Explain online and offline marketing campaigns you will execute.

Revenue Model
Where does the money come from? Who is paying?

Finances
This section is a little more in-depth and will cover the entire financial aspect of your business. Give a short introduction.

Sales Forecast

On the following charts, you will display your sales forecasts. The first chart you will represent year one on a monthly basis. In the second chart, you will represent years two and three on a quarterly basis.

Year One, Monthly

Month	Conservative Sales	Moderate Sales	Optimistic Sales
1			
2			
3			
4			
5			
6			
7			
8			
9			
10			
11			
12			

Years Two and Three, Quarterly

Year/Quarter	Conservative Sales	Moderate Sales	Optimistic Sales
Year 2/Quarter 1			
Year 2/Quarter 2			
Year 2/Quarter 3			
Year 2/Quarter 4			
Year 3/Quarter 1			
Year 3/Quarter 2			
Year 3/Quarter 3			
Year 3/Quarter 4			

Expense Budget

In this section, you will discuss the expenses your business will have. You should divide them between fixed and variable expenses. Again, you will do year one on a monthly chart, and years two and three respectively on a quarterly chart.

Year One, Monthly

Month	Fixed Expenses	Cost	Variable Expenses	Cost	Total
1					
2					
3					
4					
5					
6					
7					
8					
9					
10					
11					
12					

Years Two and Three, Quarterly

Quarter	Fixed Expenses	Cost	Variable Expenses	Cost	Total
Year 2/Q 1					
Year 2/Q 2					
Year 2/Q 3					
Year 2/Q 4					
Year 3/Q 1					
Year 3/Q 2					
Year 3/Q 3					
Year 3/Q 4					

Cash Flow Statement

These charts should depict your cash flow for the first three years. This is how much money you believe will be coming into your business, as well as how much will be going out. Year 1 will be on a monthly chart, while years two and three will be on quarterly charts.

Year One

Month	Incoming*	Outgoing
1		
2		
3		
4		
5		
6		
7		
8		
9		
10		
11		
12		

*Incoming number should be the *average* amount of expected incoming capital. (conservative + moderate + optimistic divided by 3)

Years Two and Three, Quarterly

Year/Quarter	Incoming*	Outgoing
Year 2/Q 1		
Year 2/Q 2		
Year 2/Q 3		
Year 2/Q 4		
Year 3/Q 1		
Year 3/Q 2		
Year 3/Q 3		
Year 3/Q 4		

Income Projection

The following chart should display your projected profits annually for three years.

	Year 1	Year 2	Year 3
Income Projection			

Assets and Liabilities

This chart should display your assets and liabilities to date, regarding your business. Include inventory, expensive equipment, cash on hand, debts owing, outstanding loans, etc.

Assets	Liabilities
Total	*Total*

Breakeven Analysis

Share when you intend to break even.

Unit Economics Overview

The following chart should have a guide of everything you need, including the expenses, required to open your business. (Storefront, delivery vehicle, inventory, etc.)

Cost to Open Business

Expense	Cost
Total:	(x)

Current Team

Insert all existing prominent members of your current business team here. (Managers, board of directors, etc.) as well as their resumes.

Competition

Give an honest account of your competition. Explain their strengths and weaknesses as well as how you intend to compete with them for a place in the market.

Historic Investors and Funding

Share details regarding historical investors and funding, any outstanding debt owing, and other relevant information to investments made in your business in the past.

Request

Give a detailed account of your business request, as well as what terms and conditions you intend to apply and how you intend to repay the request.

Appendix

Anything relevant to the business plan that was not relevant to a specific subsection can be included here.

Other Books by Elliot J. Smith

Available at the Kindle Store

Information at http://amzn.to/2koxLgY

Robert's Rules: The Ultimate Guide to Understanding and Practicing Robert's Rules of Order

LLC: The Ultimate Guide to Forming Your LLC in 10 Simple Steps

Passive Income: Four Beginner & Advanced Business Models to Start Creating Passive Income Online

CPSIA information can be obtained
at www.ICGtesting.com
Printed in the USA
LVHW080056080620
657632LV00010B/289